ERIN PA'   THE MU   I   MURDERER

Written by
Stu Armstrong

ISBN: 9798291610343

© Stu Armstrong Media 2025. All rights reserved.

This book is based on real events and individuals. While every effort has been made to ensure factual accuracy, certain situations, events, and dialogue have been fictionalised or dramatised for narrative purposes. No responsibility is assumed or accepted for any errors, omissions, or interpretations arising from the content of this book.

No part of this publication may be reproduced, stored in a retrieval system, or transmitted in any form or by any means—electronic, mechanical, photocopying, recording, or otherwise—without the prior written permission of the publisher.

Table of Contents

Chapter One 5
Roots in Rural Victoria 5
Chapter Two 13
The Curious Years 13
Chapter Three 22
When Two Worlds Collide 22
Chapter Four 28
Cracks in the Foundation 28
Chapter Five 33
Fractures 33
Chapter Six 38
Bitter Roots 38
Chapter Seven 44
The Poison in the Roots 44
Chapter Eight 50
The Idea Takes Root 50

Chapter Nine 57
The Beef Wellington 57
Chapter Ten 63
The Morning Of 63
Chapter Eleven 71
The Lunch 71
Chapter Twelve 78
Unravelling 78
Chapter Thirteen 83
The Walls Close In 83
Chapter Fourteen 90
The Arrest 90
Chapter Fifteen 97
Cold Walls and Colder Stares 97
Chapter Sixteen 104
The Courtroom 104
Chapter Seventeen 111
The Verdict 111
Epilogue 116
Shadows That Never Lift 116

Chapter One
Roots in Rural Victoria

On a crisp April morning in 1975, a soft breeze drifted through the open windows of the small weatherboard house on the edge of Leongatha. Inside, Margaret "Maggie" Patterson gripped her husband's hand so tightly his knuckles turned white.

"She's coming, Tom," Maggie gasped, her voice straining against the pain.

"I know, love. I know. Just breathe," Tom said, though his own heart pounded like a jackhammer.

A few moments later, the air filled with a thin but determined cry. Erin Trudi Patterson arrived just as the sun broke through the clouds outside.

"She's perfect," Maggie whispered, tears slipping down her cheeks as she held the tiny bundle to her chest.

Tom leaned over, his face cracked with a grin. "Welcome to the world, little one. You're going to do great things."

In the corner, six-year-old Mark stood awkwardly, peering at his new sister with wary eyes. "She's so small," he said. "Are you sure she's not going to break?"

"She's tougher than she looks," Maggie replied, smiling tiredly. "Just like her brother."

The house itself was modest—paint peeling on the window frames, the garden overgrown with weeds. Tom worked long hours at the service station, and Maggie had taken part-time shifts at the local medical clinic to keep up with the bills. Money was tight, but that day none of it seemed to matter.

From her earliest days, Erin was quiet and observant. While other toddlers ran wild in the garden, she preferred to sit in the shade of the big gum tree, sifting through leaves and dirt with a level of focus that seemed almost adult.

"She's not like Mark was," Maggie said one evening as she set down the dinner plates.

Tom nodded. "No, she's not. Mark's a storm, but Erin… she's more like a stream. Quiet, steady."

By the time she was six, Erin had developed a fascination with nature. She'd spend hours poking at mossy logs or collecting strange mushrooms in her little plastic bucket. On Sundays, after services at St Patrick's Anglican Church, she'd linger in the garden while the other kids ran off to play tag.

One afternoon, Reverend Grace Whitmore spotted her crouched beside a fern, gently tracing its delicate fronds with her finger.

"Do you like the plants here, Erin?" the Reverend asked, kneeling down beside her.

Erin nodded without looking up. "They're soft… and quiet. Like they're whispering."

Reverend Whitmore smiled. "You listen very well. That's a gift. God speaks in quiet ways too, you know."

At Leongatha Primary, Erin was bright but reserved. Her teachers praised her neat handwriting and keen observations in science class. She made two close friends: Jade Morris, who was loud and fearless, and Brad Collins, a quiet boy who shared her love of books.

"Come on, Erin! Stop drawing and let's play chase," Jade would call at recess, her blonde hair flying behind her as she dashed across the oval.

But Erin would shake her head, pencil in hand. "You go. I want to finish this sketch first."

"Ugh, you're no fun!" Jade laughed, running off without her.

Brad lingered nearby, peering over her shoulder. "That's a really good drawing," he said shyly.

Erin smiled. "Thanks. It's a mushroom I found near the church garden. See how the gills curve underneath?"

Brad nodded, his brown eyes wide with interest. "You could make a whole book about plants one day."

"Maybe I will," Erin said softly, tucking a loose strand of hair behind her ear.

Church was a cornerstone in Erin's young life. St Patrick's, with its whitewashed walls and stained-glass windows that caught the afternoon sun, felt like a sanctuary.

Reverend Whitmore was a gentle presence, her sermons about stewardship of the earth resonating deeply with Erin.

At thirteen, Erin joined the church's youth group, "Green Leaves," led by Mrs Eleanor "Ellie" Dane, a retired teacher with a warm smile and a habit of bringing homemade biscuits to every meeting.

"You've got a real connection with nature, Erin," Ellie told her during a creek clean-up one Saturday morning.

Erin glanced down at her mud-streaked gloves and shrugged. "It just feels… right. Like it matters."

"It does matter," Ellie said firmly. "Maybe you're meant to teach others about it."

By the time Erin entered Leongatha Secondary College in 1988, she'd grown into a tall, slender teenager with an air of quiet determination. Her love for biology flourished under the guidance of Ms Lila Asante, her Jamaican-Australian science teacher.

"You've got an eye for detail, Erin," Ms Asante remarked one afternoon, flipping through Erin's field notebook. "Have you thought about entering the regional science fair?"

Erin hesitated. "I'm not sure anyone would be interested in fungi…"

"Don't underestimate yourself," Ms Asante said with a warm smile. "Sometimes the smallest things make the biggest impact."

Socially, Erin kept mostly to herself. Jade, now vying for a spot as school prefect, accused her of being distant.

"You're always off in your own world," Jade said one lunchtime, slamming her sandwich down on the table. "Why can't you just hang out like a normal person?"

"I'm sorry," Erin replied quietly. "I just… like being outside better."

Brad, sitting beside her, shot Jade a reproachful look. "Leave her alone, Jade. Not everyone wants to be the center of attention."

Later that week, Brad caught up with Erin behind the library. "Don't listen to her," he said softly. "I think it's cool how you care about the environment and stuff."

"Thanks, Brad," Erin murmured, grateful for his steady presence.

At fifteen, Erin began working part-time at a local café to help support her family. Tom's service station was struggling, and Maggie had picked up extra shifts at the clinic.

One evening over dinner, Erin announced, "I'm going to save for university. Maybe study biology."

Tom looked up from his plate, surprise flickering across his face. "University's expensive, love."

"I know," Erin said calmly. "That's why I'm starting now."

Maggie reached across the table and squeezed her hand. "We're proud of you, sweetheart."

In December 1992, Erin graduated near the top of her class. At the school leavers' dinner, she wore a soft green dress that echoed her love for the natural world.

During her valedictory speech, her voice was calm but strong. "We leave here today not just as students, but as caretakers of the future. Every small action—planting a tree, picking up rubbish, listening—matters."

The room fell silent, then erupted into applause.

Later that night, Brad found her outside, away from the noise. "That was amazing," he said, his voice barely above a whisper.

"Thanks," Erin replied, hugging her notebook to her chest. "It feels strange… like something's ending."

"Or beginning," Brad said with a small smile.

.

Chapter Two

The Curious Years

Erin Patterson left the small town of Leongatha in the summer of 1993 with a single suitcase, her mother's parting gift a white notebook with pressed fern leaves glued inside and a growing sense of possibility.

Federation University's Gippsland campus felt like another world compared to the close-knit community of her childhood. Wide concrete paths stretched between modern glass buildings. Students lounged on grassy courtyards, laughing and gesturing animatedly, their conversations blending into a constant hum that made Erin feel both invisible and oddly exposed.

She clutched her notebook tighter as she entered the student housing block. Her new room smelled faintly of detergent and dust. The bed creaked as she sat down, staring at the bare walls.

"You're Erin, right?"

A tall, red-haired girl poked her head in the doorway, her grin wide and unselfconscious.

"Yes… I'm Erin," she said, rising awkwardly.

"I'm Tasha, your floor RA. Welcome to Manna House. Don't let the creaky beds scare you off. Everyone's going to the welcome barbecue later. You coming?"

Erin hesitated. "Maybe."

"Maybe?" Tasha folded her arms, mock-glaring. "It's not optional. Newbies eat sausages and pretend they're extroverts. It's tradition."

Erin laughed softly. "Okay. I'll come."

The first weeks passed in a blur of orientation lectures, campus tours, and late-night chats with her dormmates. Though Erin didn't naturally gravitate toward crowds, she found herself drawn to a small group of students in her biology course.

There was Sam Chen, a lively environmental science major who quoted David Attenborough with religious fervor, and Claire Jennings, an art student fascinated by botanical illustration.

"You're the one obsessed with fungi, right?" Sam teased one afternoon as they walked across the quad.

Erin pushed her hair behind her ear. "I wouldn't say obsessed. Just… fascinated."

"Obsessed in a good way," Claire added. "You talk about mushrooms like they're magic."

"They sort of are," Erin said. "They break down decay and turn it into new life. They connect whole forests underground. It's… beautiful."

Claire grinned. "You're going to be the quirky professor one day, I can already tell."

Though the university was secular, Erin's connection to faith remained strong. On Sundays she attended St Mary's Anglican, a small brick

church just off campus, with stained-glass windows depicting vines and birds.

Reverend Peter Langley, a man in his forties with wire-rimmed glasses and a thoughtful demeanor, noticed her quiet presence almost immediately.

"You're new to St Mary's," he said after service one morning. "Where are you from?"

"Leongatha," Erin replied. "I used to go to St Patrick's there."

"Ah, lovely. Reverend Whitmore's parish."

"Yes… she meant a lot to me."

He nodded. "I suspect you're the kind of person who hears God most clearly when you're surrounded by trees."

Erin smiled faintly. "Maybe."

Over time, she became involved with the church's environmental ministry. They organized litter cleanups, native plantings, and talks on sustainability. Erin often stayed late after meetings, talking with Reverend Langley about faith, science, and the quiet spaces where they intersected.

"Some people see science and God as opposites," Erin said one evening. "But for me… the more I study, the more I feel there's something bigger holding it all together."

"That's a rare gift, Erin," Reverend Langley said. "Don't let the noisy ones convince you otherwise."

University life wasn't all smooth sailing. Erin's reserved nature sometimes caused friction with louder, more social peers.

At a dorm party, she sat in a corner nursing a soda while music thumped through the walls. Tasha plopped down beside her, grinning.

"You're hiding."

"Not hiding. Just… observing."

"Right. You're going to write a novel about all of us one day, aren't you?"

Erin smirked. "Maybe."

"You should at least dance first," Tasha said, grabbing her hand.

But as Tasha tried to tug her toward the dance floor, a lanky engineering student named Daniel Hayes interjected.

"Hey, leave her alone. Some of us are allergic to crowds."

Erin looked up, startled, as Daniel dropped into the seat opposite her. He had an easy smile and a way of leaning in like he was really listening.

"You're in bio, right? I've seen you scribbling mushrooms in your notebook."

"Fungi," she corrected. "They're not plants."

"Fungi then," he said, amused. "Do you know you talk about them like they're secret agents?"

"They sort of are," Erin said, surprising herself with a small laugh.

Over the next few weeks, Daniel seemed to appear everywhere: in the cafeteria line, outside lecture halls, at late-night study sessions. Slowly, Erin let him in.

One autumn afternoon, they walked along a wooded path near the edge of campus. Leaves crunched underfoot, and the air smelled faintly of rain.

"I've never met anyone like you," Daniel said. "You're… quiet, but your head's full of life."

"Most people don't get it," Erin admitted. "They think I'm weird."

"I like weird," Daniel said, brushing his hand against hers. "Weird is interesting."

It was her first real relationship sweet, tentative, and all-consuming. They spent long evenings sprawled on the grass talking about the future. Erin confided her dream of writing a book on fungi.

"Do it," Daniel urged. "The world needs someone who sees the things nobody else notices."

But cracks soon appeared. Daniel was outgoing, always pulling her to parties, introducing her to friends. Erin often felt overwhelmed, retreating into her books and fieldwork.

"You're always in your own world," Daniel said one night, frustration creeping into his voice. "Do you even care about what's happening here?"

"Of course I do," Erin said softly. "But… it's not my world."

A week later, they parted with quiet sadness, neither quite knowing how to bridge the gulf between them.

By her final year, Erin had fully immersed herself in mycology. She spent weekends in the field, collecting specimens, cataloguing species, and writing long, meticulous notes.

Professor Alan Griffith, her thesis supervisor, praised her dedication.

"You've got something most students don't," he told her one afternoon in his cluttered office. "Patience. Precision. Passion. Don't lose it."

Erin smiled faintly. "Sometimes I think I care about fungi more than people."

"Maybe," Griffith said. "But the world needs caretakers like you."

In December 1996, Erin graduated with honors in biology. Her parents drove up for the ceremony, Maggie dabbing her eyes as Erin crossed the stage in her cap and gown.

"You did it, love," Tom said, pulling her into a rare, tight hug.

Maggie pressed a small leather journal into her hand. "For your discoveries," she said. "And your dreams."

Erin looked down at it, heart swelling. "Thank you. I'll fill every page."

As the sun set that evening, Erin stood alone outside her dorm, watching the light fade across the hills. Her journey from quiet child to budding scientist felt complete—and yet, she sensed this was only the beginning.

Chapter Three

When Two Worlds Collide

Erin wasn't looking for love when she met Simon Patterson.

It was late spring in 1997, and she had just started working part-time at a small environmental consultancy in Melbourne. The city felt overwhelming at first the screech of trams, the smell of coffee and asphalt, and the constant press of people jostling on footpaths. She missed Leongatha's quiet streets, the green hush of its trees.

Erin had settled into her small rented flat above a florist's shop in Carlton North. Most evenings she curled up with field guides or sketched delicate mycelium patterns in her journal. Sometimes she attended services at St Andrew's Anglican, though she always lingered in the back pews, listening quietly to the choir.

It was at St Andrew's that she first saw Simon.

He was hard to miss, tall, with an easy smile and dark brown hair that flopped slightly into his eyes. He was helping stack chairs after a service when Erin noticed him laughing with the vicar, his hands moving with confidence.

"Are you new here?" Simon asked when he spotted her hovering near the door.

Erin startled slightly, clutching her bag. "I... yes. I've only just moved into the area."

"Ah, a newcomer," he said warmly. "I'm Simon Patterson. And you are?"

"Erin. Erin Patterson."

Simon raised an eyebrow. "Patterson? No relation, I assume?"

Erin smiled faintly. "Not unless there's a vast clan I've never met."

"Perhaps there is," Simon said with a grin. "Well, welcome. We do coffee after the service in the hall. You should come."

"I might," Erin said, already edging toward the door.

The following Sunday she returned. And there he was again—this time pouring tea into mismatched china cups, sleeves rolled to his elbows.

"You came back," Simon said, catching her eye.

"I did."

"Good. I was hoping you would."

They talked for a while over tea about her work, his family's long ties to the church, and Melbourne's erratic weather. Erin found herself drawn to his easy confidence. Where she hesitated and overthought

every word, Simon spoke like the world had always been open to him.

Later, as she walked home under a canopy of plane trees, Erin's thoughts swirled.

He's kind. Charming. But people like him… they live in the light. I've always been more comfortable in shadows.

It started innocently enough brief chats after services, then an invitation for coffee at a little café on Lygon Street.

"You don't talk much, do you?" Simon said, stirring sugar into his cappuccino.

"I talk… just not all at once," Erin replied softly.

"I like that," he said. "Most people talk too much. You listen."

Erin looked down, a small smile tugging at her lips.

They began taking walks in Carlton Gardens, their conversations growing more fluid each time. Simon told her about his job in accounting and his dreams of one day running his own business. Erin spoke of fungi, ecology, and her belief that the smallest organisms often held the greatest power.

"Sounds like you see the world differently," Simon said one evening as they sat on a park bench watching the sun dip below the trees.

"Maybe," Erin said. "Or maybe most people just don't notice what's under their feet."

Simon reached out and took her hand gently. "I'd like to notice. If you'll show me."

Erin's heart thudded painfully in her chest.

As weeks turned into months, they began to see each other more often, dinners at small Italian restaurants, church events, and quiet evenings in Erin's flat.

One rainy afternoon, Simon showed up at her door holding a bouquet of freesias.

"You didn't have to bring flowers," Erin said, surprised.

"I wanted to," Simon replied, stepping inside. "Your place feels a bit... sparse."

"It's how I like it," Erin said, placing the flowers in a jar.

Simon watched her with a small smile. "You're different from anyone I've ever dated."

"Different how?" she asked cautiously.

"You make me slow down. You don't play games. You're... steady."

Erin wasn't sure how to respond. Part of her thrilled at his words, but another part felt an uneasy weight settling on her chest.

What if I can't be what he needs?

Their first argument came unexpectedly. Simon had invited Erin to a party at his friend's house, a lively gathering with music and laughter spilling out onto the patio. Erin lingered by the food table, feeling out of place among the confident chatter of strangers.

"You've been quiet all night," Simon said later as they walked home.

"I don't do well in crowds," Erin admitted.

"I know," Simon said gently. "But can't you try? For me?"

Erin looked away. "I'm trying. But it's... hard."

Simon sighed. "You're amazing, Erin. But sometimes I feel like you're holding part of yourself back."

By the autumn of 1998, they had been together for almost a year. Simon's friends had started making subtle comments.

"So when are you going to make it official?" one of them teased over dinner.

Simon just smiled and glanced at Erin, who shifted uncomfortably in her seat.

One crisp evening in May, Simon invited Erin to walk with him in the Royal Botanic Gardens. The air was cool and smelled faintly of eucalyptus.

They stopped by a quiet pond where ducks floated lazily. Simon turned to face her, his expression serious.

"Erin, I've been thinking... about us. About the future."

Erin's stomach fluttered nervously. "What about it?"

"I love you," Simon said simply. "And I want to spend the rest of my life with you."

He reached into his coat pocket and pulled out a small velvet box. Opening it, he revealed a delicate gold ring with a modest diamond.

"Will you marry me?"

For a moment, Erin felt the world narrow to a pinpoint. She saw Simon's hopeful face, the gleam of the ring, and her own trembling hands.

"Yes," she whispered. "Yes, I will."

Simon's face broke into a grin as he slipped the ring onto her finger. "You've made me the happiest man alive."

Erin smiled back, but deep inside, a faint whisper of unease stirred.

What if I can't live up to this?

Chapter Four

Cracks in the Foundation

Erin Patterson became Erin by name only the day she married Simon.

The wedding took place in a small church on the outskirts of Melbourne. It was a crisp October afternoon, sunlight glinting off stained-glass windows as Erin stood at the altar, her hands trembling slightly in Simon's warm grasp.

"You look beautiful," Simon whispered, his eyes shining.

Erin forced a smile. "Thank you."

The words felt strange in her mouth, almost rehearsed. She should have been swept up in joy like everyone else, but a tiny voice deep inside whispered, Are you sure?

After the honeymoon—a quiet week on the Mornington Peninsula—they moved into a modest brick house in the suburbs. The yard was overgrown, the paint slightly faded, but Simon saw potential.

"We'll make it ours," he said as they carried boxes inside.

Erin unpacked slowly, placing her field guides carefully on the bookshelf and hanging a single pressed fern leaf in the hallway. She liked the house's stillness, though at night the creaks and groans of the settling walls sometimes kept her awake.

At first, married life felt almost normal. Simon worked long hours at his accounting firm while Erin took on freelance environmental work. She also continued attending St Andrew's, volunteering with the environmental ministry and teaching Sunday school classes.

"You're settling in well," Reverend Langley remarked one Sunday. "Marriage suits you."

Erin smiled politely. But later, sitting in the quiet of her kitchen, she stared at her wedding ring and wondered if she really believed that.

In 2001, Erin gave birth to their first child, Sarah.

The labor was long and difficult, leaving Erin exhausted and emotionally raw. As she held the tiny pink bundle in her arms, tears streamed down her face—not entirely from joy.

"She's perfect," Simon said, kissing Erin's forehead.

"Yes," Erin whispered. "Perfect."

But in the weeks that followed, a heavy fog seemed to settle over her. She loved Sarah fiercely, yet felt

strangely disconnected, as though she were watching her own life from a distance.

"You're just tired," Simon said gently when he found her crying in the nursery. "It'll pass."

Erin nodded, though inside she wasn't so sure.

By 2003, they welcomed a second child, Ben, and their family seemed complete. Simon's career flourished, and he took pride in providing for them.

"Everything we need is right here," he said one evening as they watched the children play in the backyard.

Erin smiled faintly, but a nagging restlessness curled in her stomach.

Is this enough? Or am I losing myself?

As the years passed, Erin and Simon drifted into a quiet routine.

Simon threw himself into work and social gatherings, hosting dinner parties with colleagues and volunteering for church fundraisers. Erin, meanwhile, retreated deeper into her own world—gardening, sketching, and researching fungi late into the night.

"You're always out there in the yard," Simon remarked one evening, watching her from the kitchen window.

"It's peaceful," Erin replied, kneeling in the dirt.

"Peaceful's fine, but don't you want to spend time with people too?"

Erin looked down, brushing soil from her hands. "People exhaust me."

Simon sighed, running a hand through his hair. "Sometimes I feel like you're slipping away."

"I'm not slipping," Erin said quietly. "I'm just... different from you."

One Friday evening, Simon invited a group of friends over for dinner. Erin cooked a mushroom risotto—her specialty—but halfway through the evening, she felt the walls closing in.

Simon's laughter rang out as he poured wine for their guests. Erin sat at the edge of the table, fingers twisting in her lap, barely speaking.

"Erin, you're so quiet," said one of Simon's colleagues with a tipsy smile. "Don't you have any funny stories about Simon?"

Erin forced a polite laugh. "I can't think of any."

Simon shot her a look—half amusement, half frustration. Later, as they cleared the dishes, his voice was tight.

"You could have tried a bit harder."

"I was trying," Erin said. "I just... I don't like those kinds of gatherings."

"You used to at least make the effort," Simon muttered.

"I've never liked them, Simon. You know that."

One rainy night in 2005, Erin found herself flipping through an old journal, reading the entry she had written the night Simon proposed.

He's kind. Safe. He sees me when no one else does.

But now she wondered if he still saw her at all—or if she was becoming invisible in her own marriage.

Despite the growing distance, Simon still tried to reach her. On their wedding anniversary, he booked a night at a fancy hotel and surprised her with a bouquet of lilies.

"Let's get back to how we used to be," he said softly.

Erin forced a smile. "Okay."

But lying beside him that night, staring at the ornate ceiling, she felt a hollow ache in her chest.

I'm trying, aren't I? she thought. So why does it feel like I'm disappearing?

Chapter Five

Fractures

Erin Patterson had always believed marriage was a garden: if you tended it patiently enough, pulled the weeds and watered the roots, beauty would bloom.

But by the winter of 2008, she stood in the kitchen staring at a sink full of dirty dishes, and all she could see were thorns.

At first, the cracks in their relationship were subtle—small disagreements over trivial things.

"You left the light on in the lounge again," Simon said one evening as he stepped into the kitchen.

"I was going back in there," Erin replied without looking up from her chopping board.

"Were you?" His tone was light, but there was an edge to it.

"Yes, Simon. I'm not an idiot."

He sighed and leaned against the counter, folding his arms. "I didn't say you were. Why are you so defensive all the time?"

"Because you treat me like I'm... less than," Erin murmured, placing the knife carefully on the board.

Simon pinched the bridge of his nose. "Here we go again."

Not every moment was bad. There were still flashes of the old warmth—like on Sarah's seventh birthday when Erin baked a towering chocolate cake, decorating it with delicate sugar flowers.

"Wow, Mum," Sarah said, eyes wide. "It's beautiful."

Erin smiled and ruffled her daughter's hair. "Just like you."

Later, as Simon helped clear the table, he glanced at her with a faint smile.

"You've got a gift," he said quietly.

Erin looked up, surprised. "Do you really think so?"

"I do. Maybe you should start a baking business. Do something for yourself."

But the warmth faded as quickly as it came, replaced by the cold routine of work, school runs, and strained silences over dinner.

By 2010, Erin had developed a deep fascination with foraging.

It started innocently long walks through nearby woodlands, collecting wild herbs and mushrooms to experiment with in her kitchen. But soon it became something more.

"Why are you spending so much time out there?" Simon asked one Sunday morning as Erin tied her boots.

"It's calming," she replied. "I need space."

"Space from what? From me? From the kids?"

Erin hesitated, tugging at her laces. "From everything."

Simon shook his head. "You're pulling away, Erin. You're not here even when you're home."

The real rupture came later that year, during yet another attempt at a dinner party.

Erin had spent all afternoon preparing a complicated three-course meal. She'd foraged wild greens for the salad and made a mushroom tart with a buttery, golden crust.

But when the guests arrived, Simon was late. He breezed in an hour later, laughing and apologizing, carrying a bottle of wine.

"I got held up at work," he explained.

"You couldn't call?" Erin hissed under her breath in the kitchen.

"It was just an hour."

"An hour when I was panicking in here trying to keep everything perfect. Do you even care?"

Simon's jaw tightened. "Not everything has to be perfect, Erin. You drive yourself and everyone else mad with it."

They plastered on smiles for their guests, but the tension hung thick in the air.

Later that night, after the last guest left, their voices rose.

"You don't see me anymore," Erin said, tears stinging her eyes.

"Don't you see? I've been trying for years!" Simon shot back. "But you've built walls around yourself. I can't get through."

"Maybe you've stopped trying."

"Maybe I have," Simon said quietly.

Two weeks later, Simon packed a bag. "I'm going to stay with Mum for a while," he said.

Erin sat at the kitchen table, staring at the grain of the wood. "Is this it?"

"I don't know." Simon's voice cracked. "But we can't keep doing this." Sarah, now ten, stood in the doorway clutching her teddy bear. "Daddy, where are you going?"

Simon crouched down, gathering her in his arms. "Just for a little while, sweetheart. I'll see you soon."

Erin watched silently as the front door closed behind him.

The papers arrived six months later. Erin signed them with a shaking hand, the ink smudging slightly.

Her marriage of twelve years was over. She stared at the signed document for a long time, feeling equal parts grief and numbness. What now? she wondered. Who am I without him?

In the years that followed, Erin's world grew smaller. She kept to herself, pouring her energy into her cooking and foraging.

She joined a small cooking club at the church, but even there she struggled to connect.

"She's... intense," one member whispered to another after Erin launched into a long explanation about the health benefits of wild mushrooms.

At night, the house felt cavernous and silent.

Erin lay awake listening to the wind outside, her thoughts circling endlessly.

I did everything right. I kept the garden watered. So why did it still die?

Chapter Six

Bitter Roots

Erin Patterson never imagined the house would feel this empty.

After Simon left, there were still sounds—the clatter of dishes, Sarah's laughter drifting from her bedroom, Ben's thumping footsteps as he raced down the hallway. But now, silence pressed in on her like a thick fog.

It was 2012 when the children went to live with Simon.

At first, it was meant to be temporary just until Erin "got back on her feet." But weeks turned into months, and months into years.

"They need stability," Simon had said, his voice calm but resolute. "And right now, you're... not in the best place."

"They're my children too," Erin had replied, her voice rising despite her best efforts to stay composed.

"I'm not trying to take them away from you," Simon said. "But you spend more time in the woods than at home. They need someone present."

At first, Sarah and Ben visited every other weekend. Erin would clean the house meticulously before they arrived, laying out plates of freshly baked biscuits and trying to hide the nervous knot in her stomach.

"How are you, Mum?" Sarah would ask politely, sitting stiffly at the kitchen table.

"I'm fine," Erin replied, forcing a smile. "I made your favourite apple cake."

"That's nice."

But as Sarah grew into her teenage years, her visits became less frequent. She seemed distracted, her gaze flicking constantly to her phone.

"Mum, do you have Wi-Fi here?" Sarah asked one afternoon.

"No," Erin replied. "Why would I?"

"Because... it's 2014," Sarah said, rolling her eyes.

Ben, quieter than his sister, still hugged her when he arrived, but even he seemed to shrink back when Erin tried to ask about his life.

"How's school?" she asked one rainy afternoon.

"Fine," he mumbled.

"Do you like your teacher?"

"She's okay."

Erin wanted to reach out, to hold him close and tell

him she still loved him fiercely. But the words lodged in her throat like a splinter.

After one particularly awkward visit, she sat at the kitchen table long after they'd gone, staring at the crumbs from Ben's half-eaten biscuit.

They're slipping away from me, she thought. And I don't know how to stop it.

It didn't help that Simon's parents were quick to cast blame.

"I'm worried about the children," said Margaret Patterson during a tense phone call. "Simon tells me they come back unsettled after visiting you."

"They're fine here," Erin replied sharply. "I don't know what Simon's been telling you."

"He says you seem... distracted. That you've been experimenting with odd recipes."

Erin bristled. "I cook for them. That's hardly a crime."

"Perhaps not, but maybe keep things simple. Children need routine, not... whatever it is you're doing out there."

After she hung up, Erin paced the kitchen, her fists clenched.

They think I'm incapable. Even now, after all the years I gave to this family. The bitterness festered like rot.

The only thing that soothed Erin was the forest.

Each morning she pulled on her boots and disappeared into the woods, her wicker basket swinging from her arm. She learned the best spots for slippery jacks and saffron milk caps, memorized the seasons when pine mushrooms would push up through damp earth.

Her kitchen became her laboratory. Jars of dried fungi lined the shelves. Fermenting jars gurgled faintly on the counter. She spent hours perfecting stocks, stews, and sauces, testing recipes over and over.

Cooking became a ritual, a way to impose order on a world that felt increasingly chaotic. But sometimes, as she stood over a simmering pot, she wondered if the obsession was consuming her.

At least food doesn't leave you, she thought bitterly. It doesn't roll its eyes or stop answering your calls.

Her social circle, already small, began to wither. At church, people whispered about her odd habits. "She's always talking about mushrooms," one parishioner murmured. "It's a bit... much, isn't it?"

Even the cooking group she had joined drifted away. "You're very intense about food," one member said after Erin spent twenty minutes lecturing on the dangers of misidentifying wild fungi. "Maybe you should take a break."

Erin walked home that evening feeling hollow.

They don't understand. None of them ever do.

One chilly afternoon in 2015, Simon stopped by unannounced.

"I thought you might like an update on the kids," he said, standing awkwardly in the doorway.

"Come in," Erin replied stiffly.

They sat at the table sipping tea, the air thick with unspoken words.

"Sarah's doing well," Simon said. "She's thinking about university. Ben's joined the footy team."

"That's good," Erin murmured. "I miss them."

"They miss you too," Simon said gently. "But Erin... you need to meet them halfway. They don't know how to reach you anymore."

"Maybe they don't want to," Erin said, her voice cracking.

Simon reached across the table, resting his hand over hers. "You're still their mum. But you can't shut the world out forever."

Erin pulled her hand away, staring down at her tea.

That night, Erin baked a mushroom and leek pie. The smell filled the house, warm and earthy. She ate alone at the table, staring at the empty chairs. *I used to cook for them. Now I cook to fill the silence,* she thought.

As she scraped her fork across the plate, she wondered how everything had unraveled so quickly.

Maybe Simon was right. *Maybe I've built walls so high no one can climb them anymore.*

Chapter Seven

The Poison in the Roots

The silence in Erin Patterson's house was suffocating.

It wrapped around her like a wet wool blanket—itching, heavy, impossible to shake off. The ticking clock on the kitchen wall seemed louder than ever, each tick a reminder of how much time had passed since she last felt truly alive.

She sat at the kitchen table staring at her phone. No calls. No messages.

Not from Sarah. Not from Ben. And certainly not from Simon.

They all turned their backs on me, Erin thought, gripping her mug so tightly she worried it might crack.

Simon had left her nearly a decade ago, but the wound still bled beneath the surface. He hadn't just walked out of their marriage he'd taken the children too.

"They need stability," he'd said, his voice maddeningly calm as he packed his bags. "You've been... distracted, Erin."

Distracted. That's what he called it. Her long walks in the woods. Her hours spent in the kitchen experimenting with recipes.

The way she had thrown herself into hobbies because it was the only way to quiet the screaming in her head.

"You made me this way," she'd hissed at him during one of their last arguments. "You smothered me with your rules, your expectations. I'm drowning in this life you built around me."

"And yet you're still not happy," Simon had replied coldly.

The memory made Erin's jaw tighten.

He never understood me. None of them did.

Gail Patterson's voice still echoed in her mind, clipped and precise like a schoolteacher scolding a wayward child.

"I don't know how you expect the children to thrive with you in this state," Gail had said once over the phone, her tone dripping with disapproval. "Perhaps it's for the best that Simon has them for now."

"For now," Erin had repeated bitterly. That "for now" stretched on for years until Sarah and Ben stopped coming altogether.

Even Heather, Simon's sharp-tongued Aunt had weighed in, smirking over coffee during one particularly tense visit.

"Not everyone's cut out for family life, Erin. Some people just... don't have the temperament."

Erin had smiled tightly at the time, but inside her anger boiled.

The hardest part was losing Sarah and Ben.

At first, they'd stayed with her on weekends. She'd baked their favourite cakes, taken them on little adventures through the bushland, tried to make her home warm and inviting.

But slowly, the visits became shorter. Less frequent.

Sarah had started pulling away first, her teenage years making her bristle at Erin's attempts to connect.

"Mum, I don't want to go mushroom hunting again," Sarah said one weekend, scrolling on her phone. "It's boring."

"It's not boring it's educational," Erin replied sharply.

Sarah rolled her eyes. "I just want to go home."

And Ben... sweet Ben... had eventually followed his sister's lead, retreating into quiet politeness whenever he saw her.

They'd stopped coming altogether after a while. Erin told herself it was Simon's doing that he'd poisoned their minds against her.

He's always been good at that, she thought. Making himself look like the hero while I'm the villain.

Now, years later, Erin found herself alone in this house that once echoed with laughter.

Everywhere she looked, she saw ghosts. Sarah's old teddy bear, half-hidden in a cupboard. Ben's muddy football boots gathering dust by the door.

She couldn't stop the thoughts that churned in her mind like a storm.

Simon took everything from me. He charmed them all his family, our friends, even the kids. He painted me as unstable, irresponsible, unfit.

Her fingers dug into the arm of the chair.

But they don't know what he's really like. The cold silences. The subtle put-downs. The way he made me feel small every single day of our marriage.

She remembered standing in their old kitchen years ago, her hands red from scrubbing dishes, as Simon had sighed dramatically.

"I don't know why you're making such a fuss over dinner. It's not like anyone's impressed."

Impressed. That word still stung.

When Gail called out of the blue in March, Erin didn't know what to think.

"We thought it might be nice to have lunch together," Gail said. "As a family."

"A family," Erin repeated, her voice taut.

"Yes. At your place, if that's not too much trouble."

Erin's first instinct was to say no. To hang up and never speak to them again. But something in her a stubborn spark kept her on the line.

"No trouble at all," she said finally.

When the call ended, Erin sat staring at her phone, her pulse thundering in her ears.

Why now? Are they really trying to mend things—or is this just another chance to look down on me?

Over the next two weeks, Erin's thoughts became darker. Simon probably told them I'm still unstable. That I can't handle a simple meal.

She imagined them sitting around a table somewhere, planning the visit like generals plotting a siege.

"They'll come here, pick apart my home, my cooking, my life," she muttered to herself as she scrubbed the countertops for the third time that morning.

But beneath the anger, there was something else.

Maybe this is my chance. Maybe I can show them I've changed. That I'm still part of this family…

At night, Erin wandered through the empty house, her bare feet cold on the tiled floor.

She paused at the children's old bedrooms. Sarah's was still painted a soft lilac, a few faded posters curling on the walls. Ben's shelves held dusty trophies from primary school sports days.

She pressed her hand against the doorframe, her chest aching.

They're gone. And they're not coming back.

Chapter Eight

The Idea Takes Root

The house was too quiet.

It wasn't the peaceful kind of quiet, no, this silence was oppressive, clinging to Erin Patterson's skin like a damp cloth.

She sat in the kitchen staring at her phone, waiting for a call or a message that never came.

Not from Sarah.

Not from Ben.

And certainly not from Simon.

It had been years now since her family had slipped from her grasp. The kids stopped visiting. Simon moved on. His family froze her out like she was nothing more than a bad dream they were trying to forget.

She clenched her hands in her lap, nails biting into her palms.

I'm not the villain here, she told herself. But they've made me one. They took everything from me and smiled while they did it.

In the early days after the divorce, Erin had tried to forgive. She went on long walks, tried to bake her way to serenity, even joined a church group for a while. But forgiveness didn't come.

The more time passed, the more she saw the truth: Simon and his family had wanted her gone all along.

She could still hear gher former mother in law, Gail's voice as if the woman were in the room with her.

"You were never really suited to Simon," Gail had said once, her tone calm but sharp enough to draw blood.

"What's that supposed to mean?" Erin had asked, her jaw tightening.

Gail had smiled thinly. *"You're... different. Simon needs someone steady. Someone dependable."*

Steady, Dependable. Words that sounded nice but cut her to pieces.

And Heather, Simon's Aunt, had been even worse. *"Honestly, Erin,"* Heather had said over coffee one awkward afternoon, *"not everyone's cut out for marriage. Or parenting. Some people just aren't wired for it."*

The words had burned themselves into Erin's brain.

Not wired for it. That's what they all think of me.

Now, sitting alone at her kitchen table, Erin felt the weight of those judgments pressing her down.

Her children didn't call anymore. Sarah's birthday had passed two weeks ago with nothing more than a curt text message.

"Thanks for the card".

No phone call. No visit. Even the house felt like a stranger to her.

Sarah's lilac-painted room was just as she'd left it, the air stale and heavy. Ben's old football boots still sat by the back door, gathering dust.

Erin closed her eyes and tried to breathe through the ache in her chest. They're gone. Because of him. Because of them.

The idea came to her late at night, as she lay staring at the cracks in the ceiling.

It started small. What if they knew how it felt?

What if Simon, Gail, Heather and Heathers husband, Ian, what if they all felt that same crushing helplessness she lived with every day?

Would they finally understand? Would they finally respect me?

At first, the thought frightened her. She wasn't a monster. She wasn't the kind of person who hurt others. But the anger kept bubbling, rising like bile in her throat.

They've hurt me. Over and over again. Maybe it's time they felt a fraction of it.

Two days later, Erin was sitting at her laptop in the dark, her hands trembling as she typed, Deadly Australian mushrooms. Search results filled the screen:

Death cap, Destroying angel, Cortinarius, Funnel-web cap and more, her mouth felt dry as she read about their effects.

One bite can cause irreversible liver and kidney failure. Symptoms often delayed. Difficult to detect in cooked dishes. Her heart pounded.

This wasn't just a passing thought anymore. It was becoming something solid, something real.

On a crisp autumn morning, Erin pulled on her thick boots and grabbed her wicker basket. The forest was alive with birdsong, but to her it felt strangely silent.

She moved like a predator, scanning the undergrowth with sharp eyes. She knew these woods well, she'd foraged here for years, but this time was different. This wasn't about food or pleasure. It was about power.

Her fingers brushed aside leaves and moss until she saw it: a cluster of pale, ghostly mushrooms huddled beneath a log.

She knelt, her breath shallow. Death caps!

Smooth caps tinged with a faint greenish hue, delicate gills beneath. Innocent-looking to the untrained eye, but she knew better.

"Perfect" she whispered.

Back in her kitchen, Erin laid the mushrooms out on her counter. She wore gloves, her movements precise and careful and for the next three nights, she experimented.

Could she disguise the taste? Could she mask the smell?

She tried blending them into stocks, mincing them fine and mixing them with butter, sautéing them with garlic and herbs. nThe earthy aroma filled the house, but Erin's stomach churned as she worked.

If anyone knew what I was doing…

But no one would know, as no-one ever came here.

The voice in her head, each day the voice grew louder. "This is justice, this is balance, they made their choices, now you make yours"

One night, as she sat at the kitchen table staring at the jars of mushrooms, a flicker of hesitation passed through her.

What if it goes wrong? What if they die?

But the thought of Simon's smug face, of Gail's icy condescension, hardened her resolve, they don't deserve mercy.

Chapter Nine

The Beef Wellington

The scent of garlic and thyme lingered in the air, clinging stubbornly to the curtains. Erin Patterson stood barefoot in her kitchen, her hair tied back in a tight knot.

On the counter lay her weapons: a bundle of fresh herbs, a slab of beef tenderloin, and a cluster of pale mushrooms wrapped in a tea towel like a precious secret.

Her hands shook slightly as she unwrapped them, revealing the delicate white caps with their faint greenish tinge, the Death caps.

She stared at them for a long moment. They looked so harmless innocent even, but Erin knew better., this was no ordinary meal.

Journal Entry: July 28

They want lunch? Fine. I'll give them a lunch they'll never forget.

For years they've looked down on me. Gail with her polite little barbs, Heather with her smirks, Simon with that calm, patronizing voice.

But soon, they'll be the ones on their knees.

It had to be perfect. The beef wellington was her masterpiece, a showstopper, pastry golden and flaky, beef tender and blushing pink, wrapped in a rich duxelles the mushroom paste that would mask her secret ingredient.

She'd made it before, but never like this.

This time every step mattered.

They can't taste anything strange, she thought, mincing the death caps finely. No odd textures, no tell-tale bitterness.

She sautéed them slowly with butter, garlic, and thyme, the smell earthy and comforting. Comforting, she thought grimly. Perfect for putting them at ease.

"You really don't have to cook" Gail had said once, her voice sweet but edged with steel. *"We know how... complicated things are for you."*

Complicated. That word again.

"I love cooking," Erin had said, forcing a smile.

"Of course you do."

The way Gail said it made Erin want to throw the whole roast chicken she'd slaved over straight at her smug face.

Then there was Heather at last year's Christmas party. "You're still in that little house?" Heather had asked, her lips twitching. "I'd have thought you'd have moved on by now. It must be... lonely."

Erin had smiled tightly, her nails digging crescent moons into her palms. She had invited Simon as well as his parents, Gail and Donald and his Auntir and Uncle, Heather and Ian, but somin had declined the inviation saying he thought it would be uncomfortablew and awkward.

Three days before the lunch, Erin did a full test run. She seared the beef tenderloin until a golden crust formed, set it aside to cool.

Then she turned her attention to the duxelles, blending ordinary mushrooms with a small amount of the deadly caps. She cooked the mixture down until it was dark and fragrant, the liquid completely evaporated.

She tasted a smear on the tip of her finger—not enough to harm her. Delicious. Earthy. Nothing to give it away.

Next came the puff pastry, rolled thin and even. She layered prosciutto over it, spread the mushroom paste, and finally wrapped the beef inside, sealing it tight.

The oven timer ticked down like a heartbeat.

When she pulled the beef wellington from the oven, it was golden and perfect. Erin smiled, but it didn't reach her eyes.

No one would suspect a thing.

Journal Entry: July 29, 11:37 p.m.

Tomorrow's the day. I've practiced. I'm ready. They'll sit around my table, laughing, sipping wine, thinking they're safe.

And then… balance!

Erin woke early. The house was eerily still, the silence broken only by the soft hum of the refrigerator.

She moved through the kitchen like a ghost, laying out her ingredients: beef, pastry, herbs, wine.

The mushrooms were already minced and stored in an airtight container in the fridge, waiting like soldiers for her command.

She polished the wine glasses until they gleamed, arranged the cutlery perfectly.

Everything must be flawless, she thought. They'll expect nothing less.

At midday, Erin sat at the kitchen table staring at her hands. What if they realize? What if they taste something odd? What if the police come knocking?

Her stomach turned at the thought.

No. Stop it. You've planned too carefully. There's nothing to trace.

The Voice in Her Head started again, this is justice, this is your chance to take back control. After tomorrow, they'll never look down on you again.

Journal Entry: July 30, 8:02 a.m.

'Today's the day. I'm calm. Steady. They took everything from me, my children, my marriage, my dignity. Now I take something from them.'

Erin tied her apron, took a deep breath, and set to work. The pastry rolled perfectly. The beef seared to a crust. As the oven preheated, she felt an eerie calm settle over her.

This is it. There's no turning back now.

Chapter Ten

The Morning Of

The sun had barely risen when Erin Patterson opened her eyes.

For a moment, she didn't move. She lay in bed, staring at the ceiling, her heart thudding a steady, deliberate rhythm.

Today!

The word pulsed in her mind like a drumbeat.

Today is the day.

6:03 AM – Waking Thoughts

The house was cold and still. She swung her legs over the side of the bed and sat for a moment, staring at the floorboards.

Her mouth was dry. Her stomach felt hollow.

She thought of Gail, Donlad, Heather and Ian. Their voices echoed in her head, snippets of old conversations layered over years of condescension and dismissal.

"Erin, you're overreacting."

"You've never been easy to deal with."

"Maybe if you tried harder, things wouldn't have ended like this."

She clenched her fists until her nails bit into her palms. They think they've won. Today, they learn they haven't.

6:45 AM – The Kitchen Beckons

The kitchen was already spotless she'd cleaned it twice the night before—but still she wiped the counters down again.

The beef tenderloin sat in the fridge, resting like a sleeping animal.

And there, in a sealed container at the back, were the mushrooms. The Death caps. They looked harmless. Ordinary, even. But Erin knew their secret.

As she opened the fridge, a rush of cold air made her shiver. She touched the container with the tips of her fingers, half-expecting it to burn.

Careful, she warned herself. Every step matters now.

7:30 AM – A Ritual Begins

She began with the duxelles—the mushroom paste that would coat the beef inside the pastry.

Her knife moved methodically, slicing the mushrooms into fine pieces.

The air filled with an earthy, rich aroma as she cooked them down with butter, garlic, and thyme.

Erin stirred slowly, her mind humming.

They won't taste it. They won't suspect a thing. To them, it'll just be a lovely family meal.

"Lovely beef wellington, Erin" Gail would say later, dabbing at her lips with a napkin.

"You've really outdone yourself" Heather would add, her voice sweet with just a hint of mockery..

But in her mind, the scene shifted, Gail's face twisting in sudden pain, Heather clutching at her stomach, Simon's calm shattering into panic.

Erin blinked, and the image vanished. Her heart pounded harder.

8:45 AM – Doubt Creeps In

As she rolled out the pastry, Erin's hands began to sweat.

What if they taste something strange? What if they get sick too soon and connect it back to me? What if…..

She forced herself to stop.

"No. It's perfect. No one will know," she whispered aloud.

The sound of her own voice startled her. She hadn't spoken all morning.

Journal Entry: July 30, 9:02 AM

The house is quiet. Too quiet. I can feel it in my bones. This is the last morning before everything changes.

Am I scared? Maybe. But there's no stopping now. This isn't about revenge anymore. It's about balance.

9:30 AM – Paranoia Tightens Its Grip

Erin washed her hands again. And again. She wiped every surface with antibacterial spray.

She checked the oven temperature twice.

Then, on impulse, she walked to the front window and peered out through the curtains.

The street was empty except for a lone magpie hopping across the pavement.

One for sorrow, she thought, the old rhyme whispering through her mind.

10:15 AM – The Beef Takes Shape

The tenderloin was seared to perfection, its crust golden and fragrant. She let it cool as she spread the duxelles over the prosciutto on the pastry.

The beef was placed carefully on top, then wrapped tightly, sealed like a secret inside its golden coffin.

Her fingers trembled slightly as she brushed the pastry with egg wash.

It looks beautiful, she thought. No one would ever guess what's hidden inside.

10:55 AM – A Moment of Weakness

Erin sat at the kitchen table, staring at her reflection in the window. What if they die?

The thought hit her like a wave, cold and suffocating. She imagined Sarah and Ben, her children, hearing the news.

Mum poisoned them. Mum's a murderer.

Her stomach churned.

For one wild moment, she thought about throwing the beef wellington in the bin, wiping every surface, pretending none of this had happened.

You could stop now. You could still walk away. But then she thought of Gail's voice again. "Erin's never been... dependable."

And Simon's calm, patronizing tone. "You're not well, Erin. Maybe it's time to get help." Her jaw tightened.

No. It's too late. This is the only way!

11:30 AM – The Final Clean

The house was immaculate now. Erin changed into a clean blouse and skirt, brushed her hair until it shone, and dabbed a little perfume on her wrists. She rehearsed her smile in the mirror.

"Welcome, Gail. So lovely to see you." "Donald, how have you been?" The words felt wooden in her mouth, but they'd have to do.

11:58 AM – The Calm Before

The oven timer beeped softly. Erin pulled the beef wellington out carefully, the pastry golden and perfect. She set it on the counter, the scent rich and buttery, and stepped back.

Her hands were steady now. Her heart was not. She wiped them on her apron and walked to the front window. Down the street, a car turned the corner.

Her pulse quickened. They're here!

Chapter Eleven

The Lunch

The knock on the door came at precisely twelve o'clock. Erin Patterson's hands, still damp from wiping down the counter, tightened around the tea towel.

Showtime.

She smoothed her blouse, forced her lips into a smile, and pulled the door open. *"Erin"* Gail said, her voice warm but clipped at the edges.

"Gail! Donald! Heather! Ian! Come in, please."

They filed in, each carrying something, a bottle of wine, a small box of chocolates.

The air seemed to grow heavier as they crossed the threshold. Simon kissed Erin's cheek lightly, his aftershave sharp and unfamiliar.

"You've done wonders with the place" Gail said, glancing around the spotless hallway. *"Thank you,"* Erin replied. *"It's… good to see you."*

In the kitchen, Gail set the wine down on the counter. *"It smells incredible in here"* she said. *"What are we having?"*

"Beef wellington" Erin said. *"I thought it might be… special."* Gail smiled faintly. "It certainly is."

The dining table was laid immaculately: cream linen, polished cutlery, wine glasses that caught the sunlight and threw it back in scattered rainbows.

Erin watched as they took their seats, her heart hammering.

"Shall I pour the wine?" Donald offered.

"Please," Erin said.

As the red liquid swirled into the glasses, she felt her palms begin to sweat. *"Everything looks lovely, Aunt Erin,"* Heather's daughter, Sophie, said politely.

"Thank you, sweetheart."

Erin's voice sounded strange to her own ears tight and high, like a wire stretched to breaking point.

In the kitchen, she placed the golden wellington on a wooden board. The pastry was perfect: crisp, flaky, and gleaming from its egg-wash glaze. They won't suspect a thing, she thought.

She sliced carefully, laying thick pieces onto warmed plates. The smell of beef, mushrooms, and butter filled the room.

Erin paused for half a second as she spooned a portion of duxelles onto Gail's plate.

This is it…..

"Here we are" Erin said as she carried the plates in. The family murmured their approval. *"It looks divine"* said Gail. *"Absolutely beautiful"* Donald added.

As they began to eat, Erin forced herself to sip her wine. *"So, how have you been keeping?"* Gail asked.

"Busy," Erin said. *"Keeping the garden in order. Trying some new recipes."*

"Your cooking's always been… adventurous" Heather said, her fork poised delicately over her plate.

Erin smiled thinly. "*This one's traditional.*"

Erin stared down at her own plate. Eat, she told herself. You have to eat too. Otherwise they'll notice. She cut a small piece of beef, lifting it to her mouth. It tasted rich and earthy, the mushrooms melting into the meat, the pastry buttery and light.

Delicious, she thought. No one would ever guess.

As the meal went on, Erin's smile felt harder to maintain. The sound of forks against plates grated in her ears.

Heather laughed at something Ian said, and Erin's jaw tightened. They look so comfortable. So smug. As if nothing ever happened.

She caught Gail watching her. *"You're very quiet today, Erin,"* Gail said softly. *"Just taking it all in,"* Erin replied. *"It's been a long time since we were all together."*

It started with Heather. She put her fork down and pressed a hand lightly to her stomach. *"Oh,"* she said with a small laugh. *"That's odd."*

"Are you alright?" her husband asked.

"Yeah, just... a twinge. Probably eating too fast."

Erin's pulse spiked.

It's too soon, she thought. It shouldn't happen yet.

Then Gail frowned slightly. "Strange. I feel a bit... off as well." Erin set her wine glass down carefully.

"Maybe the wine's stronger than it tastes" she suggested.

"Could be" Gail murmured, though her hand hovered near her glass as if she wasn't sure.

Erin's Mask Cracks, Inside, Erin's thoughts spun wildly. This is happening. This is real.

A part of her wanted to scream, to grab their plates and hurl them into the sink, to make it stop. But another part—the colder, quieter part watched with grim fascination.

Heather stood suddenly. *"Excuse me a moment"* she said, her face pale. She left the table, moving quickly toward the bathroom. A moment later, the sound of retching echoed down the hall.

Donalds brows knitted together. *"Something's not right"* he said. He turned to Erin. *"Did you… did you use any wild mushrooms in this?"*

Erin forced a laugh. *"Wild mushrooms? No. Just button mushrooms from the supermarket."*

Donalds eyes lingered on her for a moment too long. Gail pushed her chair back slowly.

"I don't feel well either" she murmured.

She pressed a napkin to her lips and rose shakily to her feet. Erin gripped the edge of the table. Her hands were slick with sweat.

What have I done?

They're dying. It's working.

But what if they know? What if they find out it was me?

Chapter Twelve

Unravelling

Part One: Erin

The house was no longer quiet.

The sounds came in waves: Heather's vomiting in the bathroom, Gail's sharp intakes of breath, the children's frightened whispers.

Erin stood frozen in the kitchen doorway, her fingers gripping the frame so tightly they ached.

Stay calm, she told herself. You have to stay calm.

Donald was kneeling beside his wife, his hand on her shoulder.

"You're clammy" he said, his voice strained. *"You need to sit down."*

Gail shook her head, but her knees buckled.

"Something's... wrong," she whispered.

Heather stumbled out of the bathroom, her face pale and shiny with sweat. *"I've never felt like this"* she gasped. "It's not food poisoning, it's worse."

Erin forced herself forward. *"I'll call for help"* she said, her voice surprisingly steady.

She picked up her phone and dialled emergency services.

"Emergency services. Fire, police, or ambulance?"

"Ambulance," Erin said quickly. "My family they're very sick. They ate lunch here and now they're vomiting, dizzy"

The operator's calm voice cut through her panic. "Stay on the line, ma'am. Help is on the way."

As she hung up, Erin felt her stomach twist. You planned this. You wanted this.

But now, seeing their faces twisted in pain, hearing the children cry, it felt different.

What have I done?

She caught Donald looking at her again. There was something in his eyes she couldn't quite name.

Not fear. Not yet.

But suspicion.

Part Two: Ian

The pain came in waves. Ian sat on the floor beside his wife, Heather, his head swimming.

Something wasn't right. He'd had food poisoning before, this was different. Faster. More violent.

His mind replayed lunch in slow motion. Erin's careful slicing of the beef wellington. The earthy taste of the mushroom paste. Her tight smile as she watched them eat.

Did she…

The thought was so horrifying he almost dismissed it.

No. Erin wouldn't…

But then he remembered how strange she'd been on the phone when suggesting lunch.

He remembered her saying, "It's been too long," but her voice had sounded almost... rehearsed.

Heather let out a groan and slumped against the wall.

"We need to go to hospital," she said weakly.

Ian's jaw tightened.

"Yes," he said. "The ambulance is coming." His eyes flicked to Erin.

She was standing perfectly still, her hands clasped in front of her like she was praying.

Too still. Too calm.

"Erin," Ian said slowly. She blinked.

"Yes?"

"What kind of mushrooms did you use in the wellington?"

"Just... ordinary ones. Button mushrooms from Woolworths," she said quickly.

"Are you sure?"

"Yes," she said, her voice rising slightly. "Why would you even ask that?"

Ian felt his stomach twist, not from illness this time, but from dread.

What if she's lying?

The sound of sirens cut through the thick air of the house. Two paramedics burst in, their voices brisk and professional. "Who's ill?"

"All of us," Heather croaked. "We had lunch, beef wellington and now this." Erin hovered in the background, her arms wrapped tightly around herself.

Ian watched her carefully as the paramedics began assessing his wife and her sister, Gail. Erin didn't look panicked. She didn't even look surprised.

She just looked… resigned.

As they lifted Gail onto a stretcher, Ian felt a chill run down his spine. If she did this…

Why?

As the paramedics wheeled his family out, he caught Erin's eyes. For a fraction of a second, her mask slipped.

And in that moment, Ian was certain.

She poisoned us.

Chapter Thirteen

The Walls Close In

Part One: Erin – The Interview Room

The room was small and cold, the air thick with the scent of stale coffee and disinfectant. Erin sat in a plastic chair, her hands folded neatly in her lap.

A young constable stood by the door, arms crossed. Across from her, a detective in a crumpled suit flipped through a notepad.

"Mrs. Patterson, I'm Detective Hale. I just have a few questions about the lunch yesterday."

Erin forced a tight smile. "Of course. Anything to help."

"You prepared the meal?" Hale asked.

"Yes. A beef wellington. It's a family favorite."

"And what ingredients did you use?" Erin recited the list carefully: beef tenderloin, puff pastry, prosciutto, herbs, and…..

"Mushrooms?" Hale prompted.

"Yes, button mushrooms," Erin said quickly. "From the supermarket."

"Which supermarket?"

"Woolworths. I shop there every week."

Hale nodded slowly, his pen scratching across the page. "Did you do any foraging recently? Collect any wild mushrooms?"

Erin's stomach tightened.

"No. I wouldn't dare, too dangerous."

But in her mind, she saw herself crouched in the damp woods, gloved hands plucking pale caps from the undergrowth. Don't think about that. Don't let it show.

"Mrs. Patterson," Hale said, his voice even, "I have to ask directly, did you put anything in the food that could have made your guests sick?"

Erin's eyes widened in mock shock.

"Of course not! Why would I do something like that?"

Hale studied her face for a long moment.

"Why indeed," he murmured.

Part Two: Ian – The Hospital Room

The fluorescent lights above his bed made Simon squint.

His body felt heavy, his stomach raw. But the worst was the fog in his mind a thick, clinging haze that refused to lift.

"You're lucky," the doctor said softly. "We think it was amatoxin poisoning from a wild mushroom. It's serious, but you got here quickly enough."

"Mushroom poisoning?" Ian whispered. The doctor nodded grimly.

"Yes. We're treating your wife, her sister—you're your brother in law too. They're in critical care."

Ian closed his eyes. Erin made the meal. The thought rolled over him like a cold tide. She said they were button mushrooms.

But the taste had been different, earthier, more intense. He hadn't thought much of it at the time.

Now he couldn't stop thinking about it.

When the police arrived at his bedside, he wasn't surprised.

"Mr. Wilkinson," Detective Hale said gently, "we're investigating what happened. We understand a family member prepared the meal?" Ian's mouth felt dry.

"She's my newphews ex-wife," he said. "they have been separated for years." Hale nodded. "Did she seem… normal to you? Anything unusual about her behavior?"

Ian hesitated. "She was… calm. Too calm."

Part Three: Erin – The Mask Slips

Back in the interview room, Erin felt sweat prickling at her hairline. Hale leaned forward slightly. "Your ex-husband and his family are very sick, Mrs. Patterson. The doctors believe it's mushroom poisoning."

"That's terrible," Erin said faintly. "But I don't understand how"

"Are you sure you didn't forage for mushrooms recently?"

"I already told you, no!"Her voice cracked.

Hale's eyes narrowed.

"Neighbors say they saw you walking in the woods a few days ago. Carrying a basket."

Erin's breath caught. "I was collecting herbs," she said quickly. "Rosemary, thyme. Nothing dangerous."

"Hmm," Hale said. He tapped his pen against the notepad, the sound sharp and rhythmic.

Part Four: Ian – The Realization

Lying in his hospital bed, Ian replayed every moment of the lunch. Erin's smile. The way she watched them eat. The strange calm that had settled over her as Heather clutched her stomach and Gail began to sweat.

She planned this, he thought. She wanted us to suffer. He felt a surge of anger so hot it left him dizzy.

When Hale returned, Simon didn't hesitate. "I think Erin poisoned us," he said flatly.

Part Five: Erin – Cracks in the Veneer

"Why would Simon's family suggest you might have been angry with them?" Hale asked.

Erin blinked rapidly.

"We had… disagreements. After the divorce. But that's normal, isn't it? Families fight."

"Some neighbors described you as 'bitter' about the separation. About losing custody."

Erin's hands curled into fists in her lap.

"They took my children from me," she whispered. "But I would never…"

She stopped herself.

Hale leaned back in his chair, watching her. "Would never what?"

"Never hurt them," Erin said, but the words rang hollow even to her own

Chapter Fourteen

The Arrest

The knock at the door made Erin flinch. It was sharp, authoritative, and inescapable.

She froze mid-step, staring at the front door as her heart began to pound.

A second knock followed, harder this time.

"Mrs. Patterson? It's the police. Could you open the door, please?"

Erin's throat went dry.

For a fleeting second, she considered not answering—hiding in the kitchen, pretending she wasn't home, but she knew they wouldn't go away.

She smoothed her blouse with clammy hands and forced her lips into something that might pass for a smile.

Calm. You have to look calm.

When she opened the door, the morning sunlight blinded her for a moment. Two officers stood there, their faces serious. "Mrs. Erin Patterson?" the taller one asked.

"Yes?"

"I'm Detective Senior Constable Hale. This is Sergeant Ross. We're here to speak to you about the lunch you hosted last week."

"I've already spoken to someone," Erin said quickly. "I told them everything I could."

"This won't take long. But I'm afraid we need you to come with us."

Her stomach dropped.

"Come with you? Why? I—I don't understand."

Hale's voice remained calm.

"Mrs. Patterson, I'm arresting you on suspicion of administering a harmful substance. You don't have to say anything, but…."

The words blurred, her ears filled with a rushing sound like ocean waves. "This is absurd," she whispered. "I didn't do anything."

"Turn around, please."

The cold bite of handcuffs against her wrists made her flinch.

As they led her down the front path, Erin caught movement in her peripheral vision. Curtains twitching. Neighbors peeking out and someone held up a phone. Her stomach twisted.

They're filming me. I'll be on Facebook within the hour.

The backseat of the police car smelled faintly of disinfectant and old leather, Erin kept her eyes fixed on the houses flashing past each one felt like a pair of eyes staring back at her. "They're making a mistake," she murmured. "I didn't… I would never…"

Neither officer replied.

In her mind, images of the lunch replayed in fragments.

Gail's pale face. Heather clutching her stomach. Simon's eyes, sharp and suspicious.

Had she smiled too much? Spoken too little?

Did they know? Did they guess it was me?

At the police station The fluorescent lights buzzed overhead as they led her through a warren of hallways. The sound of her own footsteps seemed unnaturally loud.

It's fine. They don't have proof. They can't keep me here. But even as she thought it, her hands began to shake.

At the booking desk, they took her fingerprints and a mugshot. She caught her reflection in the polished steel of a filing cabinet, her hair was frizzy, her eyes wide and bloodshot.

You look guilty, she thought

The holding cell was colder than she expected with only a thin bench that ran along one wall. A metal toilet squatted in the corner. She sat down stiffly, wrapping her arms around herself.

The air smelled faintly of bleach and fear.

Time dragged. Erin couldn't tell if she'd been there for minutes or hours when the door opened again.

"Mrs. Patterson," Hale said. "We'd like to ask you a few questions."

The interview room was warmer than her cell but no less oppressive. Hale sat across from her, a file open on the table.

"Thank you for speaking with us again. Let's start simple, you prepared the meal?"

"Yes. A beef wellington," Erin said. "It's… a family favorite."

"And what mushrooms did you use?"

"Button mushrooms. From Woolworths."

"Are you sure?"

"Yes," she said quickly. "Why would I forage? It's dangerous." Hale nodded slowly.

"Your ex-husband believes otherwise. He says you seemed unusually calm during the meal." Erin's pulse quickened. "I was trying to be polite. It was awkward seeing everyone after so long."

Hale tilted his head. "Neighbors say they saw you walking in the bushland a few days before the lunch. Carrying a basket."

"For herbs," Erin said. "Rosemary and thyme."

"Not mushrooms?"

"No!" she snapped.

The word hung in the air like smoke.

When she was returned to her cell, an officer slid a folded newspaper through the slot.

On the front page: *"Mushroom Lunch Horror: Erin Patterson Arrested"*

Below the headline was a photo of her house, police tape crisscrossing the driveway. Erin's stomach lurched. *They've made me a monster.*

She imagined strangers scrolling through their phones, whispering in cafes:

"Poisoned her ex's family."

"She always seemed off, didn't she?"

Her cheeks burned. Everyone knows. Even Sarah and Ben…

As darkness crept into the cell, Erin lay on the hard bench, staring at the ceiling, the hum of the lights was constant and she couldn't sleep. Every time she closed her eyes, she saw Simon's face at the table. The suspicion in his eyes. The pain.

This isn't over, she told herself. I can still fix this. I just have to hold on.

But deep down, a cold voice whispered: You've already lost.

Chapter Fifteen

Cold Walls and Colder Stares

The knock wasn't a knock. It was a hammer blow.

Erin jumped, her pulse thudding painfully in her throat.

"Patterson." The officer's voice was flat, tired. "Up. Time to go."

She moved like she was underwater, legs stiff and leaden. The thin blanket fell from her shoulders, landing in a heap on the bench.

They took her shoelaces, her cardigan, and even her wedding ring—the one she hadn't worn in years but slipped on for the lunch, as though it might make her look more… maternal.

Her fingers felt naked without it.

It's only for a little while. They'll realize it's a mistake, but deep in her gut, a gnawing dread whispered: This is just the beginning.

The officers led her out through the side door of the station, but it didn't matter they were waiting.

Cameras flashed like lightning strikes. A sea of microphones surged forward. "Mrs. Patterson! Did you poison your ex-husband's family?"

"Are you guilty of murder?"

"Do you have anything to say to your children?"

She kept her head down, and her cheeks burned as a man's voice rang out above the crowd.

"You're a monster! Hope you rot in there!"

Someone held up a sign:

"MUSHROOM MURDERER."

Erin's stomach twisted violently, Sarah and Ben would see this. Her children's faces flashed in her mind, Sarah's crooked smile, Ben's shy eyes.

What will they think? Will they even want to see me again? The cuffs dug into her wrists as she stumbled toward the van.

It smelled faintly of antiseptic and old leather inside, and she thought she might vomit. Across from her sat a woman with tattoos running up her neck. "You're her, eh?" the woman said with a grin.

Erin stared at the floor.

"The mushroom bitch."

The woman laughed, a loud, hard sound.

"Cold as ice. Poisoning your ex and his old mum. Bet you'll be real popular where we're going."

Erin's stomach lurched.

At the prison gates, the van stopped with a jolt. A guard opened the door, barking orders.

"Move it, Patterson. You're not special."

The corridors smelled of bleach and sweat.

"Name?"

"Erin Patterson."

"Offense?"

"Murder. Attempted murder." The word stuck in her throat like glass.

They took her fingerprints. Photographed her. Issued her a gray tracksuit and thin plastic sandals.

"Strip." Erin hesitated.

The guard's voice snapped like a whip. "Now. We haven't got all day."

Heat rushed up her neck as she undressed under the fluorescent lights, every inch of her skin crawling with shame.

As the heavy doors to the wing clanged shut behind her, a low hum of voices rose in the air.

"That's her." "The mushroom psycho." "She killed her own family, eh?"

Eyes followed her as she walked down the corridor. A few women whispered. Others stared openly, their faces curling into sneers.

"Baby killer," someone muttered.

Erin's ears burned.

Her new home was barely big enough to turn around in. A narrow bed, a dirty thin mattress and a metal toilet bolted to the floor, The air was stale and heavy, carrying the faint scent of bleach and despair.

She perched on the edge of the bed, hugging herself.

Her mind replayed the lunch in jagged fragments.

Simon's eyes, narrow, suspicious, Heather's pale lips as she clutched her stomach, Gail's trembling hands.

Had she smiled too much? Had she given herself away?

Later, in the common area, Erin tried to keep to herself. She clutched a plastic cup of weak tea, hands trembling.

A shadow fell across her. "You're in my chair."

She looked up. The woman was tall, broad-shouldered, arms covered in crude tattoos. "I… I'm sorry." Erin slid out of the seat.

The woman smirked. "Poisoning kids? That's cold even for here." Erin swallowed hard. The woman leaned closer, her voice low and dangerous.

"Watch your back, mushroom lady. You'll get what's coming."

That evening, inmates crowded around the TV in the lounge. "Coming up next: Erin Patterson, the so-called 'Mushroom Murderer,' accused of killing her ex-husband's family with a home-cooked meal…"

On the screen, Erin's house appeared, yellow police tape fluttering in the wind.

A neighbour spoke to a reporter:

"She was odd. Kept to herself. You never know what people like that are capable of."

"She's a psycho," one inmate muttered.

Another chuckled.

"She'll fit right in here."

Erin stared at the floor, her chest tight. *The whole country thinks I'm a monster.*

Back in her cell, Erin lay on the narrow bed, staring at the ceiling. Every sound made her flinch—the clang of doors, footsteps in the corridor, distant shouts.

I didn't mean for it to go so far, but another voice whispered: "Yes, you did. You wanted them gone".

Instead, she lay rigid, the cold seeping into her bones. I'll never get out of here, she thought. Even if they don't convict me, I'm already finished.

Chapter Sixteen

The Courtroom

The sound of cameras clicking outside the courthouse was like gunfire.

As Erin stepped out of the prison van, handcuffed and flanked by officers, a wall of journalists surged forward.

"Erin! Did you mean to kill them?"

"Are you guilty of murder?"

"Why did you poison your ex-husband's family?"

The questions battered her like hailstones. Flashes of light burned her vision. She kept her head down, lips pressed tightly together.

Inside the courtroom, the air was heavy with whispers. The public gallery was packed. Erin felt every eye on her as she was led to the dock.

Opening Statements

The prosecutor, a tall man in a dark suit, rose to address the jury. "Ladies and gentlemen, this case is as tragic as it is shocking.

"The Crown alleges that Erin Patterson, in an act of malice and premeditation, prepared a meal laced with Amanita phalloides, commonly known as the death cap mushroom"

"She invited her former in-laws, Gail and Donald Patterson, and their relatives Heather and Ian Wilkinson to lunch and the result? Three dead. One fighting for his life"

"And for what? Revenge"

"Mrs. Patterson's resentment toward her ex-husband Simon and his family festered for years. This lunch was her opportunity to strike."

Erin shifted in her seat. Revenge? No. It wasn't revenge. It was… something else she thought

Her lawyer, a soft-spoken woman named Margaret, leaned over and whispered. "Don't react. No tears. No shaking your head. Just… stay still."

Erin nodded stiffly.

Simon's Testimony

Simon Patterson took the stand next, Erin felt her chest tighten. Her mind racing in tought, Will he look at me? Will he defend me?

He didn't. He kept his eyes fixed on the prosecutor.

"Mr. Patterson, can you describe your relationship with the defendant in the months leading up to this incident?"

Simon's voice was low but steady, determined, "We'd been divorced for five years. Communication was… strained. We spoke only about our children."

"Did your parents and the Wilkinsons have a good relationship with Mrs. Patterson?"

Simon shook his head. "Not really. There was tension after the divorce. Mum felt Erin blamed her for everything."

"Did Mrs. Patterson ever express animosity toward your family?"

Simon hesitated. "She said once that they ruined her life. That they treated her like garbage."

Erin's hands tightened in her lap. That's not what I said. Not like that she said to herself.

"Did you attend the lunch?"

"No. I wasn't invited."

"Did you find that unusual?" Simon's jaw tensed. "Erin never invited them to anything. So yes. It was strange."

Ian Wilkinson's Testimony

When Ian Wilkinson entered the court, Erin's breath caught. He walked with a cane, his face gaunt, skin pale and the room fell silent.

"Mr. Wilkinson," the prosecutor began gently, "can you tell us what happened on the day of the lunch?"

Ian's voice was hoarse. "We were invited to Erin's house. Gail said it was an attempt to mend fences."

"What was served at lunch?"

"Beef wellington. Erin said it was her specialty."

"Did anything seem unusual about the meal?" Ian's eyes flicked toward Erin, then away.

"Not until after, maybe ann hour later, Heather said she felt sick. Then Gail. Then Donald, I felt it too, a pain in my stomach like nothing I've ever experienced. We were all vomiting."

Ian's voice cracked. "I watched my wife die, she screamed my name… then she was gone."

Erin closed her eyes, her stomach churning. I didn't mean for them to suffer, not like that she whispered to herself

Cross-Examination

Margaret stood slowly, smoothing her skirt. "Mr. Wilkinson, are you aware that Mrs. Patterson denies ever foraging for wild mushrooms?"

Ian's jaw tightened. "I don't believe her."

"You're not an expert in mycology, correct?"

"No."

"Could it have been an accident? A case of store-bought mushrooms being contaminated?"

Ian shook his head firmly. "It wasn't an accident.

Erin's Inner Monologue

As witness after witness took the stand, Erin felt herself shrinking. They've all decided. I'm guilty. In their eyes, I might as well have pulled a trigger.

The prosecutor's words echoed in her mind. "Premeditation. Malice. Revenge."

The Media Frenzy

During a recess, Erin caught a glimpse of a newspaper through the glass of her holding cell.

"MUSHROOM MURDER TRIAL: THE LUNCH THAT SHOCKED AUSTRALIA"

Her own face stared back at her,m pale, hollow-eyed, her mugshot splashed across the front page.

Closing the Day

As court adjourned, Erin's legs felt like lead. Margaret touched her arm.

"You did well. No outbursts. That's good."

"Are they going to convict me?" Erin whispered.

Margaret's mouth tightened. "It's too early to say. But we have work to do."

As she was led back to the prison van, the shouting began again.

"Witch!"

"Killer!"

"Rot in hell!"

Erin kept her head down, but inside, her thoughts screamed.

I didn't mean to kill them. I just wanted them to hurt for once… she spoke to herself

Chapter Seventeen

The Verdict

The courthouse was a hive of murmurs and shuffling feet. Erin sat rigid in the dock, her hands folded tightly in her lap. A sheen of sweat coated her palms.

The jury had been out for eight hours.

Eight hours of imagining, over and over, how they saw her: a grieving ex-wife, or a cold-blooded killer.

From outside came the muffled roar of voices. The media circus had only grown since the first day of her trial. Australia's most hated woman, one headline had screamed.

"Jury's coming back," whispered Margaret, her lawyer. Erin's stomach dropped.

This was it…..

The courtroom filled quickly. Simon Patterson sat in the second row, flanked by his sister and a cousin. His face was pale, eyes sunken.

He didn't look at Erin. Not once.

Behind him, reporters scribbled furiously in their notepads.

The jury filed in. Twelve faces Erin had studied for weeks now masks of unreadable calm.

The judge nodded gravely.

"Madam Foreperson, has the jury reached a verdict?"

The forewoman, a middle-aged woman with short hair and a steady voice, rose.

"We have, Your Honour."

"In the matter of the charge of murder of Gail Patterson, how do you find the defendant?"

"Guilty."

Erin flinched, the word hit her like a slap.

"In the matter of the charge of murder of Donald Patterson, how do you find the defendant?"

"Guilty."

Her breath came shallow, her heart pounding so hard it felt like it might burst.

"In the matter of the charge of murder of Heather Wilkinson, how do you find the defendant?"

"Guilty."

Her vision blurred. This can't be real.

"And in the matter of the charge of attempted murder of Ian Wilkinson, how do you find the defendant?"

"Guilty."

⊔

Erin's Inner Monologue

No… no, no, no… nShe wanted to scream. To stand up and shout that they were wrong. Instead, she sat frozen, her fingernails digging crescents into her palms.

Margaret put a hand on her arm. "Stay calm. Don't give them what they want." But Erin barely heard her.

The words guilty, guilty, guilty echoed in her skull like a drumbeat.

Simon's Perspective

Simon closed his eyes as the verdicts were read.

Justice, but it didn't feel like victory. His mother was gone, his father, his Aunt Heather And Erin… Erin had destroyed herself.

He remembered the first time he'd seen her, laughing at a church youth barbecue. How had they gotten here?

As Erin was led from the dock in handcuffs, she heard the roar of reporters outside.

"Erin! Do you have anything to say?"

"Do you regret it?"

"Will you apologise to Simon and his family?"

The lights of cameras flashed like lightning as guards hustled her into the waiting van.

Back at the women's prison, news of the verdict spread fast. "That's her, the Mushroom bitch, guilty, eh? Good!"

Inmates jeered as she was escorted down the corridor. "You'll never get out." "Psycho."

Alone in Her Cell that night, Erin sat on the edge of her narrow cot, staring at her hands, ashw was yet to be sentenced, but the least she could hope would be Thirty years., 'I'll be in my seventies before I even have a chance she thought'. Tears slid down her cheeks, silent and hot.

On the television in the common room, her own face flashed up on the news again.

"MUSHROOM MURDERER FOUND GUILTY"

Meanwhile hiding in her cell, she curled up on the bed, pulling the thin blanket tight around her shoulders, but even in the darkness, she couldn't escape the sound of that word echoing in her head.

Epilogue

Shadows That Never Lift

The cell was cold, even after six months in prison, Erin still woke each morning expecting to be at home in Leongatha, the kettle boiling, the sound of her children's footsteps on the stairs.

But there was no home. No kettle. No children.

Just the thud of boots on concrete, the smell of bleach, and the jeering voices of women who had already decided she deserved worse than this.

She sat on her bed, staring at the tiny window where a slice of pale sunlight tried to break through the bars.

This isn't real, she thought, though she knew it was.

The Ghost of a Life

Her children hadn't visited. Not once. A single note had arrived weeks after her conviction, scrawled in Sarah's hesitant handwriting:

We're safe. Staying with Dad. Please don't write!

Erin read it so often the paper had begun to tear at the folds. She kept it under her pillow, taking it out at night to trace the words with her fingers.

They're scared of me, she told herself. But they don't hate me. They can't.

In the prison yard, she was a curiosity. Women watched her as though she were some exotic animal locked in a cage. *"That's her,"* one inmate muttered, *"Mushroom lady, Should've given her the needle."*

On her worst days, Erin wondered if they might make good on those whispered threats. She'd heard stories of boiling sugar water thrown in faces.

Maybe that's how she'd leave this place burned, scarred, another name in the system.

The Weight of Guilt

At night she replayed the lunch over and over, Gail's laughter at the table, Heather offering to help with the dishes, Donald complimenting her Beef Wellington.

An hour later they were groaning in agony.

Ian had looked at her then, not with anger but confusion. "Why… why would you…?" Erin had no answer. She still didn't.

Margaret, her lawyer, had told her to keep a journal. "It'll help you process," she'd said.

Erin tried.

'I never meant to kill them. I just wanted them to feel what I felt—abandoned, betrayed.'

'Was it really murder if I didn't mean for them to die?'

But deep down she knew those were excuses.

The World Moves On

In the outside world, life went on. Netflix announced a documentary: *"Death Cap: The Leongatha Mushroom Murders."*

A podcast dissected her every move: *"Erin's Recipe for Revenge."*

Tabloids ran with lurid headlines:

*"**BEHIND BARS: MUSHROOM KILLER'S PRISON HELL.**"*

Even Simon spoke once, briefly, to a reporter. "She'll never hurt anyone again," he said. But his voice lacked triumph. It was weary, broken.

The Final Blow

The day that the verdict delivered was a blur, "*Erin Patterson,*" the judge intoned, *"you have been found guilty of three counts of murder and one count of attempted murder.*

The words echoed in her head still, night after night. Thirty years, she had been told was best case scenario, that would make her seventy-four before she even had a chance at freedom, that's If she lived that long that was.

Author's Reflection

At the time of writing, Erin Patterson has been found guilty on all charges:

- Three counts of murder (Gail Patterson, Donald Patterson, Heather Wilkinson)

- One count of attempted murder (Ian Wilkinson)

She has yet to be sentenced, but all indications point toward life imprisonment with a minimum term of thirty years. It's doubtful Erin will ever be released. Even if she survives her sentence, what would await her on the outside? A family that no longer exists? A world that has branded her forever as *"Australia's Mushroom Murderer"?*

Through research for this book, it became clear Erin was a complex woman. To some, she was just *"a bit odd"* a quiet, socially awkward figure. To others, she was manipulative, cold, and capable of something truly monstrous.

But did she deserve to lose her children? Was that devastating loss the final trigger that pushed her over the edge?

Or was this outcome always inevitable, was she de4stined to kill?

Was Erin someone with murder in her DNA, carrying a darkness that only needed the right spark to ignite?

I can't answer those questions. Nobody truly can, not even Erin herself. But they're certainly food for thought.

When a parent loses their children, whether through tragedy, estrangement, or legal action, it can drag them into a very dark place.

But the key question here is: were Erin's children taken from her by her former husband Simon, unfairly and out of spite? Or did Erin's own behaviour push them away? Was their removal warranted for their own safety, or is that something we tell ourselves because it fits the narrative?

What is undeniable is the devastation Erin's actions have left in their wake.

She has torn apart two families.

Shattered the faith of her small-town community and church, and perhaps worst of all, destroyed the lives of her own children.

Sarah and Ben will grow up in the shadow of this crime. They will likely carry the scars forever, children of the woman who killed with mushrooms.

Whatever you believe about Erin Patterson, monster, victim, or something more complicated none truth remains:

Some wounds never heal.

The End

www.stu-armstrong.com

This book is part of Stu Armstrong's 'True Crime + series' make sure to check out more titles from Amazon, Kindle, Audible and Apple iBooks or visit www.stu-armstrong.com

Printed in Dunstable, United Kingdom